Unleash your limits to find success

Author's Biography

Abderrahmane Dakir was born in Casablanca in Morocco. Since graduating from University Hassan II

he has worked in international companies since 1998 as Web Engineer. In 2003, he founded and now manages his own company 1NEWLOG.

Since January 2015, he started writing short-stories in English in order to share his ideas about life, family, nature with the rest of the world.

Wisdom tooth is just an example to write about patience with ourselves, with others and with God. In this short story the dentist becomes our 'patience coach', helping us to hold back and not give in too quickly to pain and suffering.

Preface

Abderrahmane Dakir very concisely ties together the effects of the limits we can put on ourselves on our life's journey to success that we seek. Although he acknowledges, in his short story, that no one is born with the skills and talents that make them successful later in life, he does highlight the fact that only some people are born with a strong internal link to an inner motivation that Mr. Dakir suggests is also linked to a universal and higher strength that aids us and pushes us forward.

So take Mr. Dakir's advice and unleash your limits and become someone who can inspire and pass these important keys to success onto future generations.

Sonia Cooke
English teacher native speaker

Could we maintain all the exciting feelings we experience after achieving life goals?

How many times have you felt boredom in your life?

"If you are bored with life, if you don't get up every morning with a burning desire to do things - you don't have enough goals."
Lou Holtz.

I would always spend on material things that I wanted and needed to enjoy myself. But after having getting them, I started to feel an emptiness in my spirit such as a gap that I could not fit myself in anymore.

The only thing that can satisfy my feelings is learning new things whether they are related to my field or not.

My spirit needs to feel replenished in order to overcome boredom that is often created by seeing the same place, listening to the same songs, watching the same movies, reading the same books. Even though they are always very good.

In fact, to feel better our spirit seeks out new adventures and explores our vast space and that's why human beings try to discover the universe more and more. Sing different songs, write different books, act in different movies, travel in and around many countries to enjoy themselves in the limitless diversity available.

To take an example, in the healthcare field, doctors spend all of their lives researching to find suitable medicines for some diseases. Each day for them is one step forward. So, they wade in limitless research.

In addition, in nature, there are tons of fish, animals, birds, flowers, trees, natural resources that we mine for, that's why many fields of science have been created to spend all our life in deep study, learning as much as we can about them.

Whatever the aspect of nature, science, business, movies, songs...etc, they are all just there for us to enjoy ourselves and to fulfill our spirits that require constant replenishment with new things to overcome the boredom that so easily descends upon us from time to time.

It goes without saying that people who know how to live each and every single day to its fullest, experience real joy and they don't do anything that is less than their very best. Since they set the day's goal, week's goal, months' goal, year's goal, life's goal ahead of time. As a result, they are absolutely successful people.

I have chosen one person called Miloud Chaabi who inspires me a lot and pushes me to stay on a straight track, even after his passing in April 2016.

My best friend Ahmed had an opportunity to met him at a lecture in a high school. The director of this high school had invited Mr. Chaabi to teach the students about the keys to success and when my friend told me about him, it made us both feel proud as he represents the model entrepreneur of our country.

Let us travel back in time to Miloud Chaabi's beginnings: "It was a hard year in the small village called Chiadma near the coastal city of Essaouira in the south of Morocco. There was a drought and water supplies had almost all dried up in all of the wells in that village.

It was so hard to feed a family or to nourish the animals and livestock too. In the midst of these circumstances, a child called Miloud was born in 1929 in the poorest village in Morocco.

In his early life, he was given the responsibility of keeping, taking care of and tending to the sheep. One day when he was playing with his friends, a wolf ate one of his family's sheep.

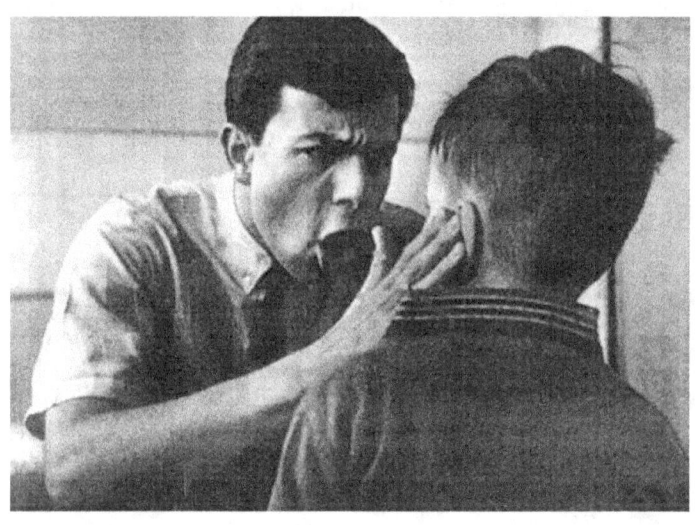

He was afraid to return back home since his father had a tough character. He would kill him in that case. Therefore, he caught a bus that took him from Chiadma to Kenitra : a city in the mid-north of Morocco.

All the first, he tried to find a shelter, he asked a manager of a construction site whether he could take shelter in the building that was under construction. The manager had the mercy on Miloud because he was still a child. He stood up for him and allowed him to sleep there as long as he could satisfy some errands of buying some food to the employees such as eggs, tomatoes, and bread every day.

As a child, he was very smart, he started to buy the eggs directly from the supermarket that was much further away, instead of buying them from the grocery that was just round the corner of the building in order to save some money for himself.

The next day he had an even better thought and he resolved to buy chickens to have free eggs.

Later, he even used his ingenuity to buy a bike to quickly deliver meals to all the construction workers that worked near of that district.

He had grown up in the hardest of lands and that's why he never hesitated about his any decisions. He forged ahead and he never looked back. He kept his goals in the forefront of mind. He challenged himself each and every day to achieve his daily goals.

Whatever goals he gave to his subconscious mind, he would work night and day to achieve them.

He knew very well where he was, where he was going and where he wanted to be. Even his thinking was big, he thought for himself.

He constantly, consistently and purposefully envisioned his goals over and over again to start to make decisions that led him straight to his goals.

Later, he founded his own company that created new jobs and boosted our economy, though he preferred to hire candidates who had a high level of education in order to reach an international level, since he had never had the opportunity to learn in any schools. He was raised in a poor family, so his family didn't have money to send him to school as the other families did with their children.

He would seek out competent candidates to hire with problem-solving skills and critical-thinking skills and he would pay such employees more than he would pay his own son. All matters are related to finding dedicated and talented persons who can indulge in their job, respect deadlines and can apply their knowledge to projects and therefore come up with the insights to be a leader in that field.

No one is born good at everything. Miloud Chaabi became good at such things through hard work. His sign of strength was asking for help, this fact allowed him to learn something new everytime.

With his team, he would write down, to high degrees of clarity, what their goals were on a regular basis to help his team to achieve them. Then, God's force came to their aid.

They came to understand that no business could run without things being written down. As the saying of Anais Nin :"If it is not written down, it doesn't exist."

Their goals were big but not supernatural. Then, they put together step by step strategies to transform their achievable goals and turn them into reality.

Setting and achieving goals was a great motivator.

The rush they felt every time they checked one of those goals off the list would inspire them to accomplish even more of them.

They always produce tangible results. Sometimes, the results could be an abundance of money.

He also founded an organization to help the people. He gave a monthly amount of money to the poor in his hometown.

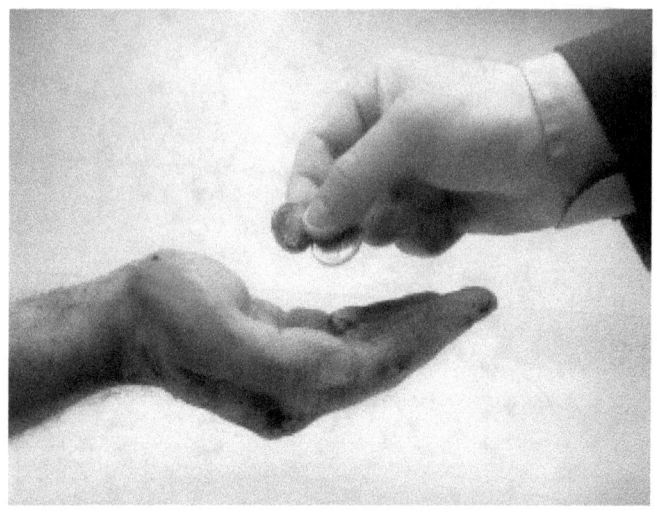

To recognize the efforts of women he called his huge company Yenna Group after his mother's name.

Throughout the course of sixty years of hard work, he also possessed a great secret strength; he always got up before the dawn to start early his job and slept early in the evening.

In 2012 his photo was portrayed on the cover of Forbes magazine as the richest man in our country. He had started from scratch to become the number one in all the businesses he set up.

In April 2016, he died before achieving all of his goals since he always set the goals in the short and others in the long terms.

He challenged himself everyday to live moments to the best of his ability and to their fullest; challenges that were based on the newest and most limitless goals."

My childhood was better than Miloud Chaabi's was, because I didn't have to think about whether I could go to school, whether I would have a house to live in or whether my neighborhood was safe to play in. However, right now, he has contributed and created a lot more than I have for others. What will my contribution be?

Maybe when we lose one thing we understand how valuable it was. In the same way that when things are handed to us we don't understand its value either, even when and especially when it's our parents who are giving us these things. It is so easy to be given something but not so easy to work for it.

Our God gives us knowledge, money, mercy unlimited in order to make us responsible for teaching more students, giving more money to the poor and being more kind towards others.

Once we relate ourselves to the one of limitless capacity our perspectives change.

Instead of competing with limits, we could collaborate to build healthy relationships that could be based on respect and love.

So our hearts become bigger and have the biggest capacity to fit everybody in through love.

At the end of the day, thinking in limitless terms is in you, since you have been created to live in joy and change your life for the better with each and every single day's goals. None of it will matter unless you relate your joy to the One who gives us limitless creativity, limitless ability, limitless capacity, limitless love, limitless mercy, limitless resources, limitless universe, and the limitless goals of each day.

www.ingramcontent.com/pod-product-compliance
Lightning Source LLC
Chambersburg PA
CBHW071328310526
45789CB00016B/1868